Disgusting Body Facts

Itches and Scratches

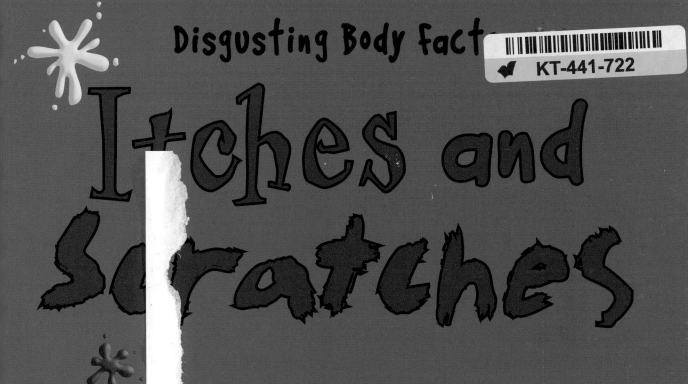

Angela Royston

Raintree

www.raintreepublishers.co.uk
Visit our website to find out more information about Raintree books.

To order:
☎ Phone 0845 6044371
🖨 Fax +44 (0) 1865 312263
📧 Email myorders@raintreepublishers.co.uk

Customers from outside the UK please telephone +44 1865 312262

Edited by Nancy Dickmann, Sian Smith, and
 Rebecca Rissman
Designed by Joanna Hinton Malivoire
Original illustrations ©Capstone Global Library 2010
Original illustrations by Christian Slade
Picture research by Tracy Cummins and Tracey Engel
Originated by Capstone Global Library Ltd
Printed and bound in China by Leo Paper Products Ltd

ISBN 978 1 4062 1307 2 (hardback)
14 13 12 11 10
10 9 8 7 6 5 4 3 2 1

ISBN 978 1 4062 1313 3 (paperback)
14 13 12 11 10
10 9 8 7 6 5 4 3 2 1

British Library Cataloguing in Publication Data
Royston, Angela.
  Itches and scratches. -- (Disgusting body facts)
  1. Itching--Juvenile literature. 2. Skin--Diseases--
  Juvenile literature.
  I. Title II. Series
  616.5-dc22

Acknowledgements
We would like to thank the following for permission to reproduce photographs:
Alamy pp.**11**, **17**, **20** (©Medical-on-Line), **15** (©imagebroker/Kurt Möbus), **23** (©Bart's Medical Library/Phototake Inc.), **26** (©Nic Cleave Photography); Getty pp.**9** (©National Geographic/Darlyne A. Murawski), **21** (©Bill Beatty), **29** (©Darlyne A. Murawski); iStock-photo.com p.**28** (©Ales Veluscek); Photo Researchers, Inc. pp.**19**, **27** (©Dr. P. Marazzi), **25** (©SPL); Shutterstock pp.**7 bottom** (©Oberon),**12** (©Alan C. Heison), **13** (©Jessica Bethke); Visuals Unlimited, Inc. p.**7 top** (©Dr. Dennis Kunkel).

Cover photograph of a healing wound reproduced with permission of Photo Researchers, Inc. (©Edward Kinsman).

Every effort has been made to contact copyright holders of material reproduced in this book. Any omissions will be rectified in subsequent printings if notice is given to the publishers.

All the Internet addresses (URLs) given in this book were valid at the time of going to press. However, due to the dynamic nature of the Internet, some addresses may have changed, or sites may have changed or ceased to exist since publication. While the author and publishers regret any inconvenience this may cause readers, no responsibility for any such changes can be accepted by either the author or the publishers.

Some words are shown in bold, **like this**. You can find out what they mean by looking in the glossary.

Contents

Itchy skin

Skin covers almost all of your body. Skin keeps out dirt and **germs** that can make you ill. It protects you from the sun. However, skin can sometimes itch. It can itch so much it drives you crazy!

Did you know?

Scratching can stop skin itching, but scratching can also make things worse. This book will tell you why.

5

Itchy head

Your head itches when your **scalp** is itchy. Your scalp is the skin below your hair. Your head may itch when you have:

- insects in your hair called head lice
- **dandruff**
- dirty hair and scalp
- shampoo left in your hair.

dandruff

6

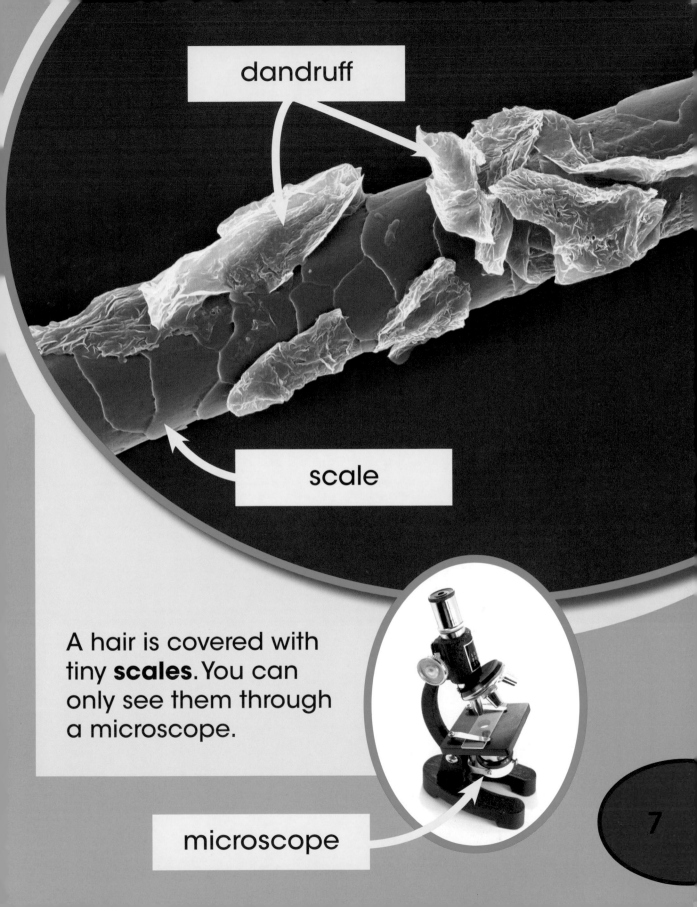

dandruff

scale

A hair is covered with tiny **scales**. You can only see them through a microscope.

microscope

Head lice

Head lice are insects that live in your hair. They bite your **scalp** and suck up some of your blood. The lice's **saliva**, or spit, makes your head itch. Their poo makes your head itch, too!

head lice

hair

Did you know?

Head lice lay lots of eggs. The eggs hatch into more lice. Soon your whole head could be crawling with lice!

Dandruff

Your skin loses flakes of dead skin all the time. The flakes are too small to see. You get **dandruff** when the flakes clump together. They form big white flakes. Dandruff makes your **scalp** itch.

dandruff

The more this person scratches, the more dandruff she makes!

11

Sunburn

Too much sun harms your skin.
Sunburn makes your skin dry and itchy.
Large pieces of dead skin peel off.

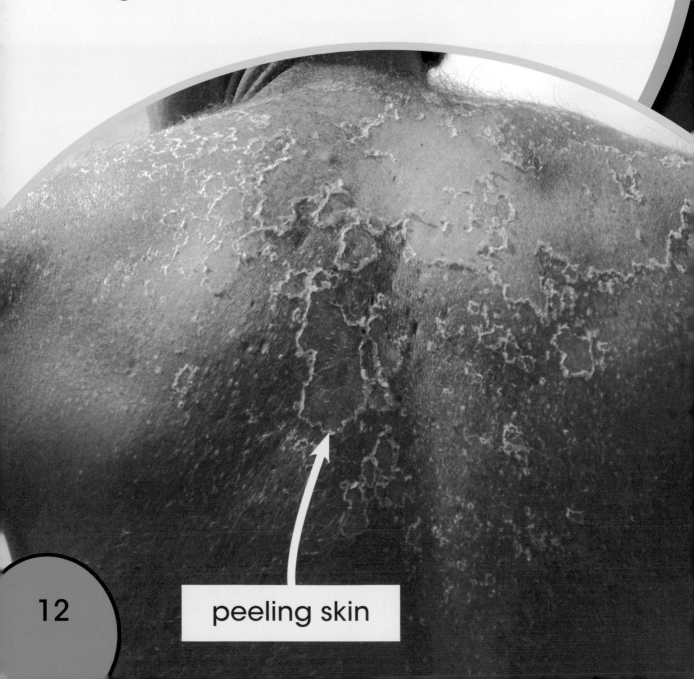

peeling skin

sunburn

(!) WARNING

Sunburn is bad for your health. It can cause a dangerous disease called **skin cancer** when you are older. When you are out in the sun, remember to cover your skin and protect it with sun cream.

Heat rash

If part of your body is often hot and sweaty, you may get a heat **rash**. Lots of small red bumps will appear on your skin. A heat rash is very itchy!

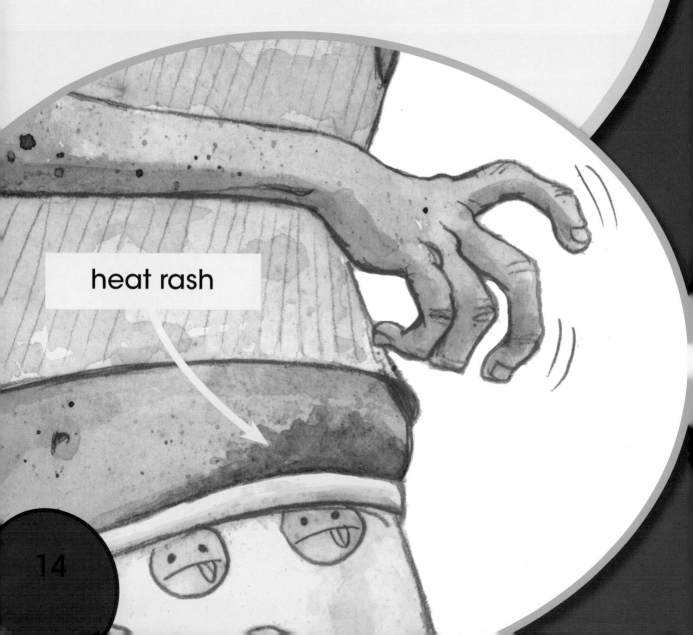

heat rash

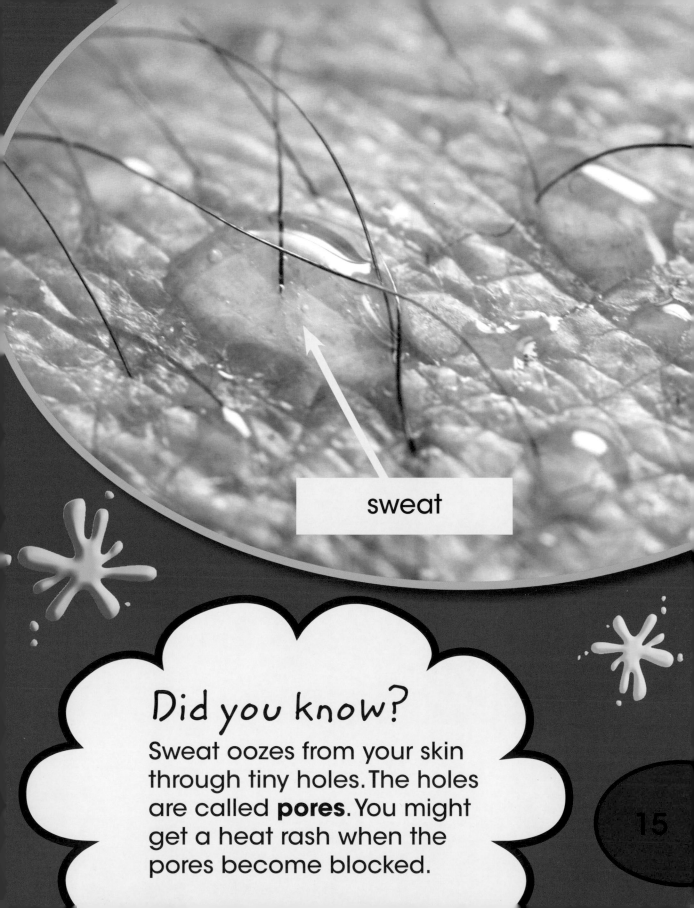

sweat

Did you know?

Sweat oozes from your skin through tiny holes. The holes are called **pores**. You might get a heat rash when the pores become blocked.

15

Skin allergy

Some people have a skin **allergy**. The allergy gives them itchy red marks called a **rash**. The rash may include little **blisters**. Scratching makes the rash worse.

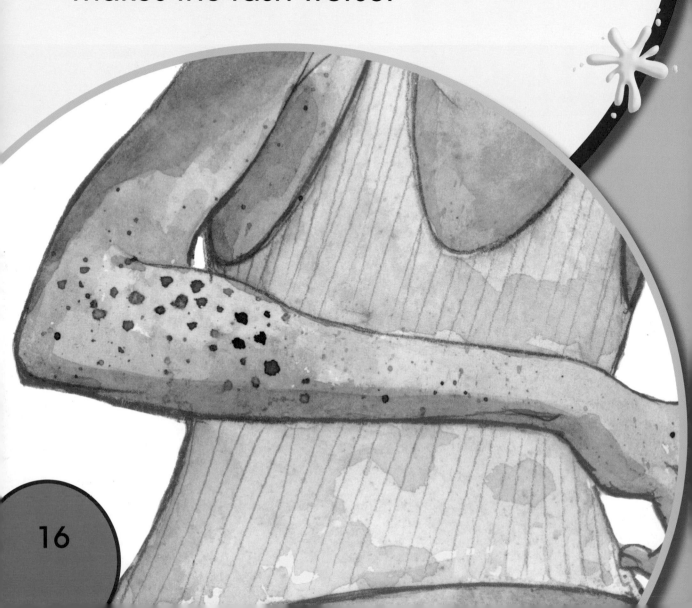

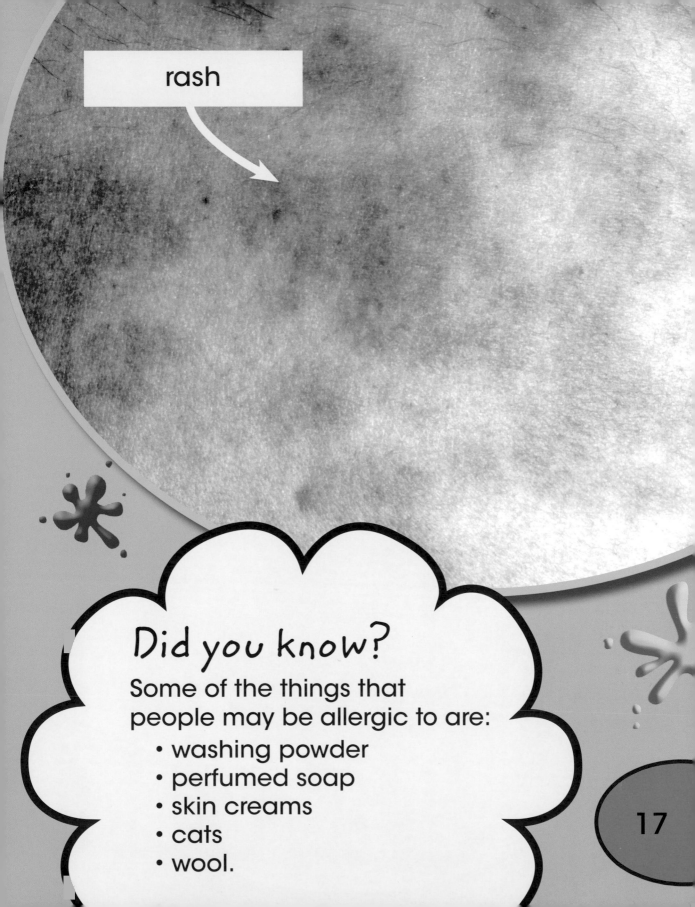

rash

Did you know?

Some of the things that people may be allergic to are:

- washing powder
- perfumed soap
- skin creams
- cats
- wool.

Food allergy

Some people are **allergic** to certain foods. For example, eating peanuts may give them an itchy **rash**. The rash is often red and blotchy.

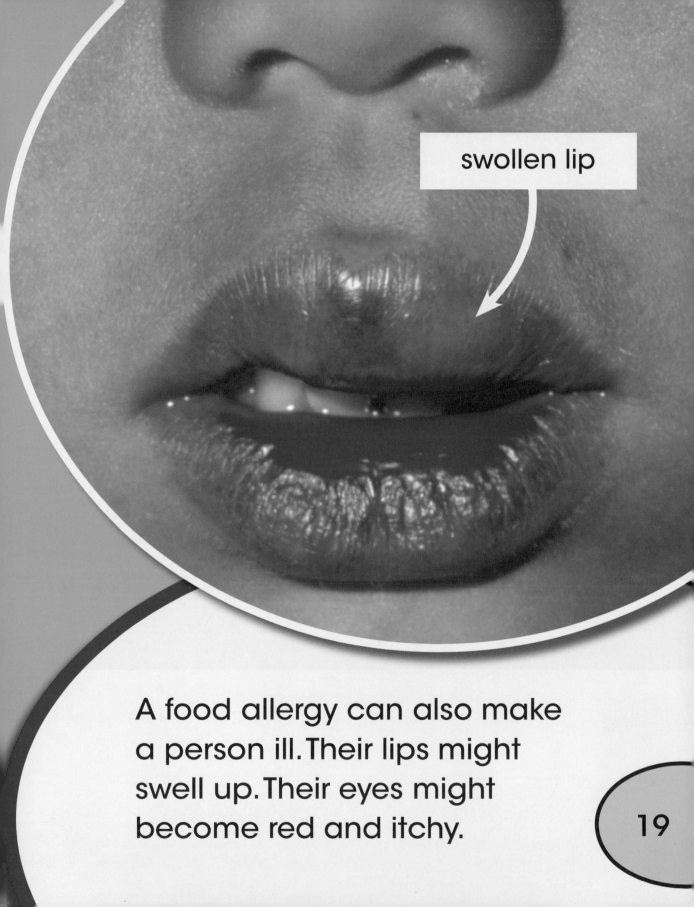

swollen lip

A food allergy can also make a person ill. Their lips might swell up. Their eyes might become red and itchy.

19

Chicken pox

Chicken pox is an illness. You can catch it from someone who already has it. Chicken pox gives you an itchy **rash** on your body. Little red bumps change into **blisters**.

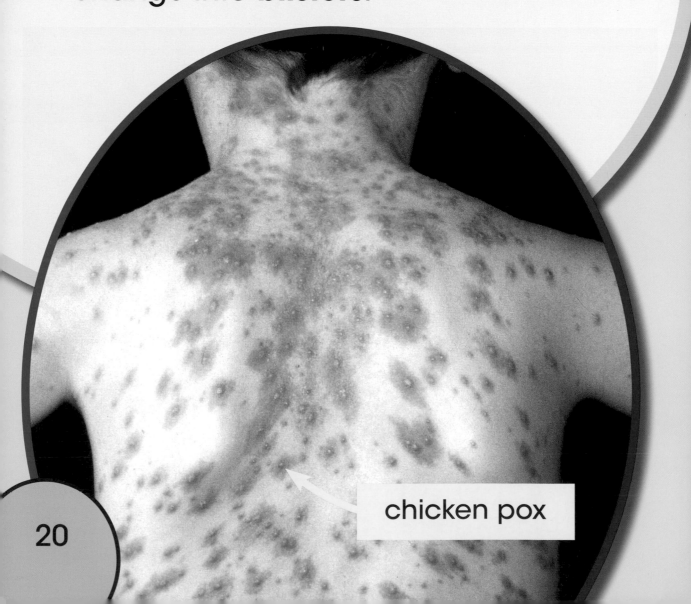

chicken pox

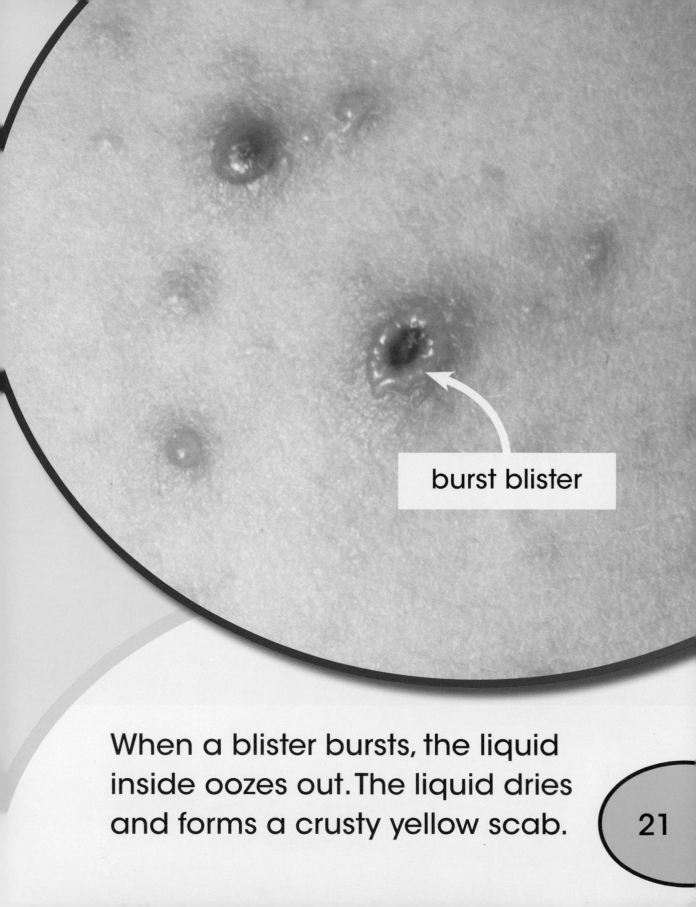

burst blister

When a blister bursts, the liquid inside oozes out. The liquid dries and forms a crusty yellow scab.

21

Warts and verrucas

Warts are catching, too. They are caused by **germs**. The germs get into your skin through tiny cracks. A wart forms a bump on your skin. It can last for months.

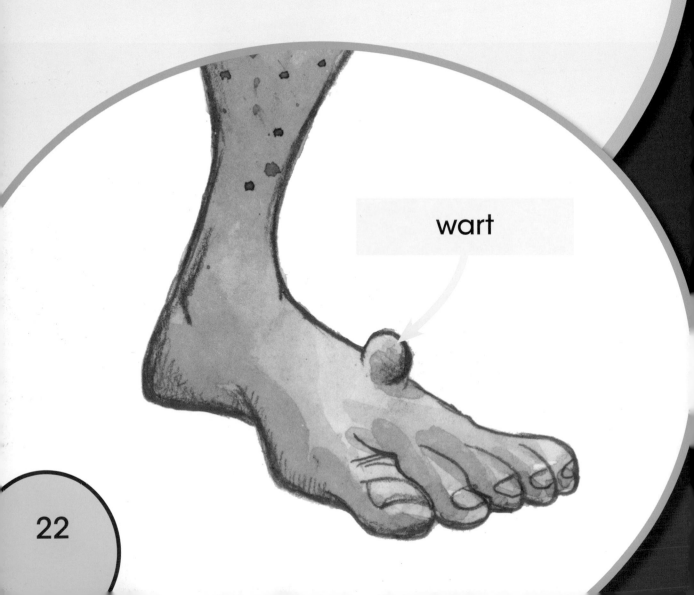

wart

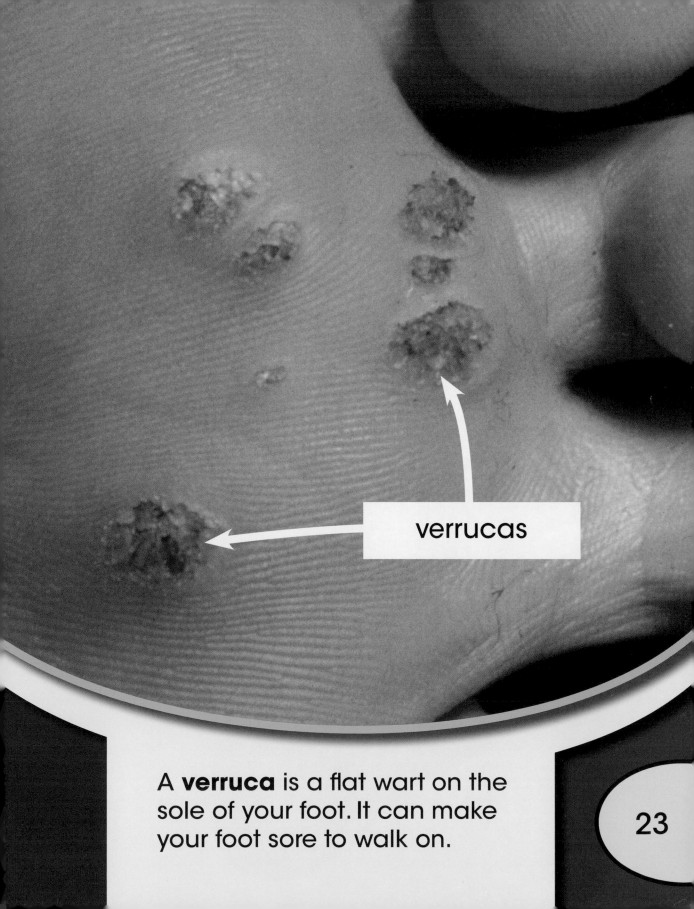

verrucas

A **verruca** is a flat wart on the sole of your foot. It can make your foot sore to walk on.

Athlete's foot

Athlete's foot makes the skin between your toes itchy and **scaly**. Athlete's foot is caused by a **fungus**. A fungus is a small living thing, a bit like a plant.

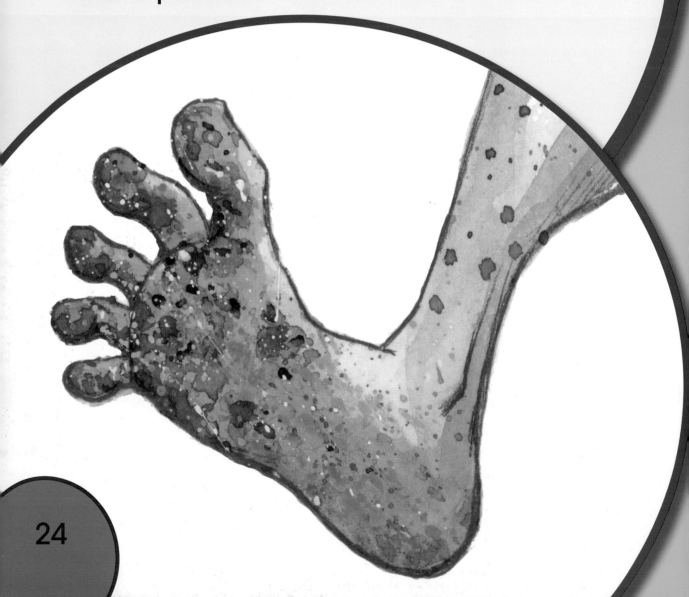

Did you know?

You can catch athlete's foot from someone who has it. You are most likely to catch it if your feet are often hot and sweaty.

This is a magnified photo of someone's toenail. You can see the athlete's foot fungus in red.

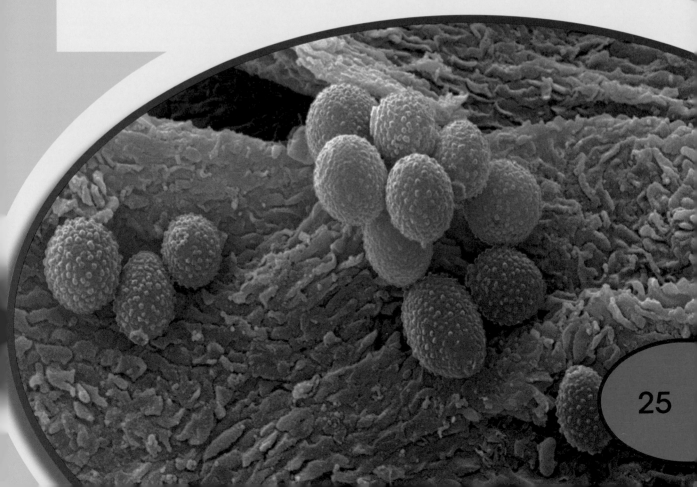

Scratching

Scratching can make a skin problem much worse. When you scratch, your nails scrape across your skin. Your nails make tiny cuts in your skin.

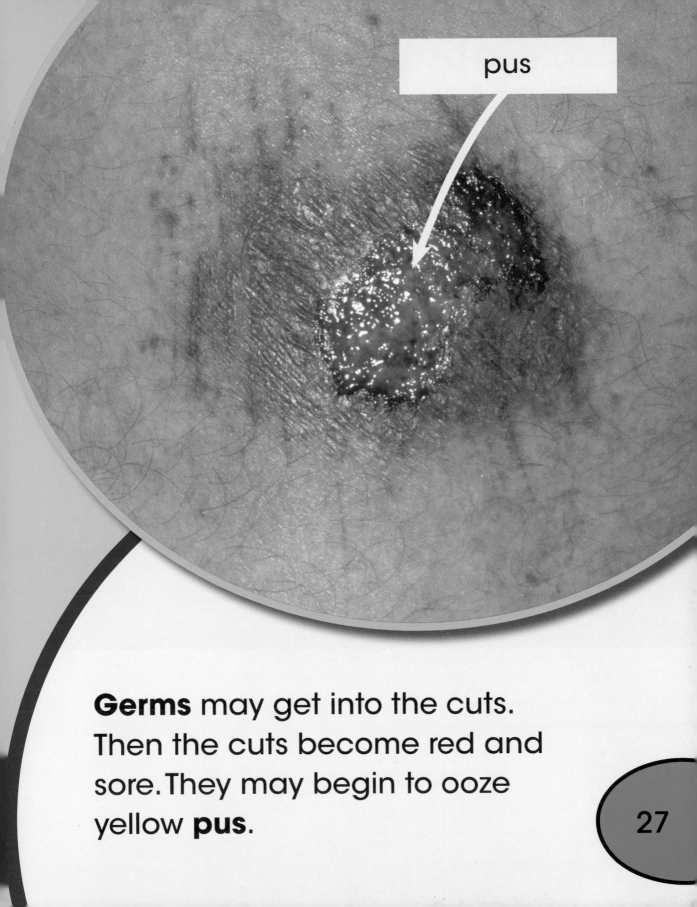

pus

Germs may get into the cuts. Then the cuts become red and sore. They may begin to ooze yellow **pus**.

More about skin and hair

The thinnest skin is on your eyelids.

Fine hairs grow all over your body. But they do not grow on the palms of your hands or the soles of your feet.

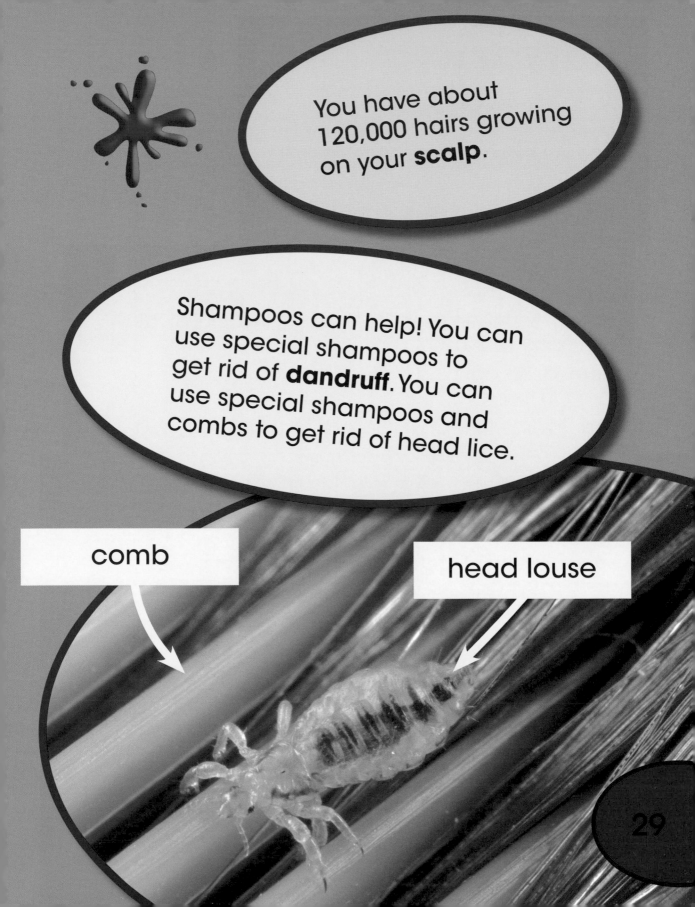

You have about 120,000 hairs growing on your **scalp**.

Shampoos can help! You can use special shampoos to get rid of **dandruff**. You can use special shampoos and combs to get rid of head lice.

comb

head louse

Glossary

allergy when you are very sensitive to something and your body reacts badly to it

blister a swelling on the skin that is filled with liquid

dandruff white flakes of dead skin that form on your scalp

fungus a small living thing. Mould and mushrooms are types of fungus.

germs tiny living things that can make you ill if they get inside your body

pore a tiny opening in the skin. Sweat escapes through pores.

pus thick yellow or white liquid that forms when a cut is infected by germs

rash red marks on the skin. Rashes can sometimes be itchy.

saliva liquid in the mouth. Saliva is also called "spit".

scale a small, flat, hard piece of skin that protects the body

scalp the skin on the top and back of your head. Hair grows from your scalp.

scaly covered in scales

skin cancer a type of dangerous disease

verruca a type of wart. Verrucas usually grow on people's feet.

Find out more

Find out

Can pets get head lice?

Books

How's Your Health? Allergies,
Angela Royston (Franklin Watts, 2006)

My Best Book of the Human Body, Barbara Taylor
(Kingfisher Books, 2008)

Up Close: Human Body, Paul Harrison
(Franklin Watts, 2009)

Websites

kidshealth.org/kid/health_problems/index.html
Go to "Skin" to find out more about athlete's foot,
eczema, rashes, and other skin problems.

**www.evelinakids.nhs.uk/kids/health/illnesses/
h/head_lice.html**
The Great Ormond Street Hospital's website for
children that tells you all about head lice.

www.headlice.org/kids/index.htm
This website is full of facts, games, animations, and
poems about head lice.

Index